EIGHT WHEELERS
in Colour

First published in 1995
by Roundoak Publishing
Nynehead, Wellington, Somerset,
England TA21 0BX

© Copyright 1995 **Peter Davies &
Roundoak Publishing**

ISBN 1 871565 24 3

Design: Peter Davies

Typesetting: Character Graphics, Taunton

Printed by The Amadeus Press,
Huddersfield, West Yorkshire

Front Cover: Loaded high with reels of tissue,
this 1959 Seddon DD8 and Crane drawbar
trailer captures the atmosphere of road haulage
in the Sixties as it toils its way over Shap on the
new M6 motorway. This 32-ton outfit featured the
classic Gardner 150 engine, David Brown
gearbox and Kirkstall drive axles and was part
of the celebrated Athersmith Bros' fleet from
Barrow-in-Furness. The picture is repeated on
page seven.

Lorries Illustrated

EIGHT WHEELERS

in Colour

A 1953 AEC Mammoth Major Mk.III tipper from the fleet of Sam Anderson of Newhouse
One of Britain's finest eight wheelers in one of Britain's finest liveries

Peter Davies

Roundoak Publishing

Preface

This book portrays a full colour pictorial record of Britain's best known eight wheeled lorries exactly as they were seen at work during the Sixties and Seventies. Through the camera of a dedicated lorry enthusiast it captures real life working vehicles, affording the reader a unique opportunity to revisit those halcyon years when the UK transport scene was dominated by home produced lorries from such famous manufacturers as AEC, Albion, Atkinson, Guy and Scammell.

The pictures are not set up but are spontaneous records of real life situations as they occurred. The quality of the photographs varies since many of the earliest colour shots were taken on a rudimentary camera with none of the modern day luxuries of zoom lens, automatic metering or auto focus. All adjustments had to be guessed and often in a hurry in order to grab a quick shot of a lorry on the move.

Not surprisingly, with the limited exposure latitude of transparency film, some shots are also a little under or over exposed but, where the vehicle justifies it, they have been included as possibly the only existing record. The author extends his thanks to the many operators for allowing access to their premises and to fellow enthusiasts and drivers who have helped with information.

Peter Davies
Flitwick. August 1995

Contents

Holt Lane 'Atkis' were a legend in their own right and this very early Defender, almost indistinguishable from a Mk.II-cabbed Black Knight, was brand new when photographed at the company's yard in Prescot, near Liverpool in 1969.

Introduction

The one aspect of a commercial vehicle which possibly captures the imagination more than anything is the livery. After all, were it not for the livery, all lorries of one type would be virtually identical. What sets one company's vehicles apart from those of another are the colour, signwriting and registration number.

As time passes so liveries change. Some disappear from the scene altogether and others are modernised to reflect the taste of the period. Many famous liveries have already faded into history unrecorded. Others have only been recorded in monochrome.

Transport liveries often reflect the culture of a country - they can be flashy and elaborate or discreet and refined. Britain has its own style, even though the variety within that overall style is considerable.

One class of vehicle which dominated the British transport scene for decades is the eight wheeled rigid. Whilst still popular today for certain types of operation, the "rigid eight" was at its peak in the early post-war years up to the late Sixties.

Few vehicles can look quite as impressive as a nicely liveried rigid

eight. In spite of many legislative changes aimed to encourage the use of artics the British eight wheeler is still a viable machine on certain traffics.

In this book we look back on some of Britain's finest eight wheelers of the post-war era, brought to life in full colour. Such legendary names as Holt Lane Transport, R Hanson, BRS, Sutton's and Tayforth are just a few examples of the famous liveries featured.

Certain makes feature more prominently than others, reflecting the numbers in operation. AEC, Atkinson, ERF, Foden and Leyland were by far the most common makes in use during the period this book covers. Albion, Bristol, Maudslay, Seddon and Thornycroft were all declining in numbers as far back as the Sixties. Dodge were in the eight wheeler market but briefly.

This book sets out to record a cross section of the most popular types, including the AEC Mk.III and Mk.V, the Leyland Octopus in its many guises from the 22.O/1 to the Ergomatic and such classics as the "bow front" Atkinsons and S18 cabbed Fodens. It also, hopefully, conveys a positive image of the lorries which perform a vital role in the nation's economy.

The haulage industry, in spite of its importance to the quality of modern day life, receives precious little appreciation from the general public. Indeed most press coverage tends to be adverse. On occasions lorries have become the target of public abuse. Rarely does the industry defend itself or try to educate those who exhibit anti lorry tendencies. Few such people stop to think how important the rapid reliable movement of goods is to our everyday creature comforts.

Were it not for the service provided by our haulage industry the supermarket shelves would be empty, the filling stations and pubs would run dry, no houses could be built and no newspapers or milk would arrive on our doorsteps.

Far from being regarded in such a bad light lorries should be respected and applauded for the benefits they bring. People in the industry, from drivers and mechanics to traffic clerks and transport managers, should equally be applauded for the demanding jobs they do. Should the haulage industry shut down for just a day or two the effects would immediately be felt.

Enthusiasts and most people in the transport industry have a greater appreciation of lorries and their importance. Not only do lorries perform a vital role, they are in themselves fascinating examples of engineering. The diesel engine, gearbox, axles, braking, steering and suspension systems are all beautifully designed mechanisms which function in unison, often for thousands of miles without attention.

A well designed machine of any sort is a joy to watch and lorries are no exception. Just as we can find time to admire the workings of a steam locomotive so we should those of a heavy lorry. The modern lorry deserves the greatest admiration of all. It is expected to carry up to 25 ton loads at sustained speeds of 60 mph for hours on end. It can be called upon to clock upwards of 150,000 miles a year - that's 15 times the mileage of a typical family car.

Outwardly lorries can be painted in magnificent liveries and many are works of art in their own right. One can only trust that in the fullness of time the lorry will receive the public admiration it deserves. Preserved vehicles are increasing in numbers and it is rewarding to see well attended displays of classic lorries in many parts of the

Athersmith's Seddon, a classic from the Fifties

country. Thanks to many dedicated enthusiasts our transport heritage will not be forgotten. Perhaps this book will inspire an even greater awareness of the significance of liveries when restoring the lorries of yesteryear.

AEC

AEC Ltd., Southall, Middlesex

The Associated Equipment Company of Southall pioneered the internal combustion engined rigid eight wheeler with the launch of their Mammoth Major 680 model in 1934. The company, famous as the builders of London's buses, went on to build eight wheelers throughout their history which ended when the factory was closed in 1979.

AEC introduced an improved, lighter version of their Mammoth Major, the O386 Mk.II, in 1935. This served as the blueprint for their famous Mk.III which appeared in 1948. This featured a more powerful 125bhp 9.6 litre diesel and full air braking.

A complete redesign took place in the Fifties culminating in the launch of the Mk.V in 1958. AEC took over the Maudslay Motor Company of Coventry, themselves builders of rigid eights, in 1948 and Crossley Motors of Stockport in 1949 to form the ACV (Associated Commercial Vehicles) Group.

Thornycroft, another well known eight wheeler manufacturer, joined the group in 1961. ACV was swallowed up in 1962 by its rivals British Leyland, who already owned Albion and Scammell.

From 1964 and the launch of the Ergomatic tilt cab AEC and Leyland eight wheelers looked almost identical but were mechanically quite different. The Ergomatic Mammoth Major was the last type of AEC eight wheeler to be marketed and underwent numerous specification changes during its production period between 1964 and 1977. From 1972 onwards they were predominantly built as 30 ton gvw machines. A lightweight Marshal rigid eight with the AV505 engine was offered between 1967 and 1968.

Above: Seen loading at Arrow Bulk Carriers, Hull is an ex-Shell Petroleum Mammoth Major Mk.III dating from 1957. It has a sliding door cab by Park Royal Vehicles and a 4000 gallon tank. The vehicle was part of a large fleet operated by A E Evans, Regent Transport of Barking, Essex.

Right: This earlier 3871 Mk.III from 1953 features the Holmalloy all-metal cab popular with British Road Services. It is loaded with Perkins engines for Commer Karrier at Dunstable and was one of a number based at Peterborough Depot.

TROWBRIDGE
SHEFFIELD LTD
CONTAINER SERVICE
TROWBRIDGE
TROWBRIDGE
SHEFFIELD LTD
TRANSPORT
ROAD T TRANSPORT
ROAD T TRANSPORT
4
25
WWA 849

Left: Trowbridge Transport of Sheffield ran an impressive fleet of AEC eight wheelers, operating a trunk service to London and the South East. This 1956 model is a particularly fine example with its lift-off container body, pre-dating the arrival of standard ISO containers.

Right: A load of steel from Colvilles of Glasgow is the cargo for this 1959 '3873' flat from the large Dundee based fleet of Allison's Freightlines. Popularly referred to as the 'Tin Front' this was the last type of Mk.III built.

Left: Large capacity eight wheeled vans are particularly impressive vehicles. Prior to entering the fleet of Herman Tideswell of Kingsley, Stoke-on-Trent, this 1958 Tin Front ran on the Firestone Tyres contract with Fisher Renwick Services. The improvised radiator blind was a common sight in cold weather years ago.

Above: Launched in 1958 as the successor to the Mk.III, the Mk.V Mammoth Major featured a radical redesign. Eight wheel brakes were an option although this one, dating from 1962, still had six wheel braking which saved on unladen weight. It is from the fleet of F Hannaby of Wrexham, on contract to Marshall Refractories.

Left: The Interconsult 'double bubble' cement tankers of the Tunnel Portland Cement Company were built on 14ft 8in wheelbase Mk.V chassis with Duramin cabs. This example, one of a small number based at Pitstone Works near Ivinghoe, is seen in the old grey livery which was changed to red in the late Sixties. Note Tunnel's personalised radiator badge.

Above: One of the largest AEC fleets in the UK was that of the London Brick Company. The majority of their Mk.Vs had distinctive RTS cabs with forward opening doors but this one, dating from 1959, was one of an early batch supplied and features a more conventional Park Royal style cab.

Left: A heavy duty body and sturdy front shunting jaw give this 1966 24 ton gross 'Ergo' a solid appearance befitting a vehicle used on plant transport. It belonged to the large nationally based Wimpey Construction concern. Both this and the Whiteley vehicle *(opposite)* have door-mounted rear view mirrors while later Ergos had them mounted on the A pillar.

Right: Though departing entirely from the traditional AEC image when launched in 1964, the Ergomatic tilt cab Mammoth Major became a lasting favourite among lorry enthusiasts. It was the first significant joint development after Leyland took over AEC in 1962. B S & W Whiteley of Pool in Wharfedale, Yorks, operated a fleet of AECs to distribute their products which included waxed papers for electrical coil windings.

Left: After weight legislation changes in 1972 rigid eight wheelers could run at 30 tons gross. This 1975 Shell Oil (UK) tanker designed for the maximum legal weight and powered by an AV760 diesel was photographed delivering to a rural filling station in mid-Bedfordshire.

Above: Leyland Group rationalisation saw the axeing of AEC as an independent marque in 1979. In the late Seventies AEC eight wheelers were already declining in numbers. The last few were built in 1977 and some bore 1978 T-suffixed registration numbers like this smart example from the Leicestershire based fleet of Charles Draper. It was photographed near Oadby in July 1979.

ALBION

Albion Motors Ltd, Scotstoun, Glasgow

Albion entered the eight wheeler scene with their T561 model in 1936 but soon developed their better known CX7 range which appeared in 1937 and continued in production through to 1951. An improved model, the HD57, with more powerful engine appeared in that year.

Following the takeover by Leyland Motors, eight wheeler production was curtailed, since the HD57 was a direct rival to Leyland's own Octopus. However, in 1957, it was decided to launch a new lightweight Albion eight wheeler in the form of the Caledonian. This utilised the Leyland 600 Series steel cab and O.600 diesel with Leyland 5-speed gearbox. Axles, suspension and frame design were all of Albion origin.

Caledonians were built for a relatively short period up to 1962, just after the Leyland LAD Octopus was launched. A lightweight LAD Octopus embodied Albion Reiver hub reduction axles from 1964.

The only other excursion into the eight wheeler field by Albion involved the lightweight Cameronian - basically a Reiver with a second steering axle added. It was aimed mainly at the export market but a handful went into operation in the UK.

Above: The CX7N was the archetypal Albion rigid eight. It retained its old-fashioned appearance until 1951 when it was replaced by the more modern flat-fronted HD57. This van bodied CX with Duramin cab began life as a tanker with Guinness before passing to B R Mills of Chesterfield, in whose livery it appears here.

Right: Still operating in the Guinness fleet and photographed in its native Liverpool in 1966, this 1954 HD57 is loaded with demountable export bulk tanks. It too has a Duramin cab.

Left: In 1957 Leyland put Albion back into the eight wheeler market with the Caledonian. It had the O.600 engine like its Octopus counterpart but featured Albion axles and air-over-hydraulic braking. Road Services (Forth) operated a number of Caledonian bulk liquid tankers, SWG826 being a typical example dating from 1961.

Above: Though mainly intended for the Australian market, the lightweight Cameronian was sold in limited numbers in the UK. It was, to all intents, a Reiver with an additional steering axle. Although not badged as such, this tipper has a similar specification to the Cameronian. It started life with Hoveringham Gravels in 1967 and was later operated by an owner driver in the Rugby area for Tarmac Ltd.

ATKINSON

Atkinson Lorries Ltd., Walton-Le-Dale, Lancashire

Atkinson, once a famous steam lorry builder, was re-formed in 1933 to concentrate on diesel lorries. It entered the eight wheeler market in 1937 with the L1586 – a classic 'assembled' lorry using Gardner, David Brown and Kirkstall running units. It remained in production with little change until 1952. AEC engines were used when Gardners were in short supply during the war.

An improved L1586, popularly referred to as the 'Bow Front', came on the scene in 1952 and by the late Fifties a fibreglass cab with wrap-round two piece screen was introduced. At 24 tons gross the models became L1786 (or S1786 for short wheelbase tippers).

A lightweight version, the Weightmaster, was announced in 1962. In the early Sixties Atkinson tried to modernise their image with the 'Bodyline' cab (popularly called the 'tin front') which concealed the traditional exposed radiator, but customers preferred the old style.

In the mid-Sixties designations became based on gross weight (eg L2486) and eight wheelers were dubbed 'Black Knight' or 'Gold Knight'. The former were haulage chassis and the latter tippers or mixers. A taller version of the Mk.I fibreglass cab, dubbed the Mk.II, appeared in the late Sixties.

Atkinson was bought out by Seddon in 1970, virtually coinciding with the appearance of the new Defender. The last Defenders were produced in 1975 and were superceded by the Seddon Atkinson 400.

Above: Atkinson L1586 eight wheelers were launched in the late Thirties and remained virtually unchanged until 1952. This handsome panelled-in tanker dates from 1951 and ran in the fleet of Dalton & Co Ltd from Belper, Derbyshire, the makers of Silkolene lubricants. Its styling has been enhanced by a Foden front bumper.

Right: Traditional style liveries set any eight wheeler off to good advantage and this fine Gardner engined 'Bow Front' from 1955 looks particularly handsome in the red and blue colours of Stoke-on-Trent based John T Heathcote Transport.

Left: No less attractive than Heathcote's vehicle (p. 25) is this 1956 'Bow Front' L1786 from the noted eight wheeler fleet of J E Parker, Malinbridge, Sheffield. With its neatly roped and sheeted load of paper reels it is a classic 'eight legger' from the golden era. It is powered by a Gardner 6LX '150', hence the wide radiator.

Above: Atkinson's new Mk.I fibreglass cab with its two-piece wrap-round screen made its debut in 1958 but the traditional 'Bow Front' cab continued for some years after that. The new cab is featured on this nicely liveried flat from Darwen based Harwood Meggitt. Loaded with steel sheet it is shod on old style 40x8 tyres.

Left: Photographed in Brigg, Lincolnshire, this L2486 Mk.I was part of a large fleet of petroleum tankers operated by Texaco. It dates from 1963.

Right: Parked up in the busy yard of Holt Lane Transport, Whiston, Prescot is a 1964 L2486 flat with drawbar trailer. Holt Lane was one of the best known operators of eight wheelers and trailers and one of the last to operate such outfits. They hauled cable and related products for the giant BICC works at Prescot.

Left: The 'tin front' or 'Bodyline' cab appeared in 1963 but was never built in any great volume. Seemingly most operators preferred the solid, traditional exposed radiator. Beecham's Foods was one company that operated the type. This 1963 example was photographed on the M1 near Toddington Services in May 1970.

Right: From about 1964 the Mk.I cab was modernised to take four headlamps, a feature which had appeared on the 'tin front' in 1963. Atkinson also began naming their models, this one being a 1967 'Black Knight' in the famous livery of R Hanson & Son of Wakefield.

Left: Another well known name in the Yorkshire area was Cawoods of Doncaster, who operated this 1968 Gold Knight with Gardner 6LX engine. This was the last type to feature the Mk.I cab, the taller Mk.II version being introduced on all models from 1969.

Right: The first Defenders appeared in 1970 as 24 and 26 ton gross models but the 30 ton gross versions soon followed when weights went up in 1972. This brand new 30 ton Defender tipper was photographed at the RHA Tipcon convention in Blackpool in May 1973. It subsequently put in over 20 years' reliable service with its one owner, T R Hughes of Holywell, Flintshire. Power unit was a Gardner 6LXB '180' giving the required 6bhp per ton.

Left: Last of a famous line of eight wheelers from the Sutton & Son fleet in St Helens was this 30 ton gross flat, WDJ217M, new in 1973.

It was retired in 1988, marking the end of an era for Sutton's fans. The St Helens firm operated one of the most celebrated Atkinson eight wheeler fleets in the country.

Right: This smart limestone bulker is pictured at the Chapel-en-le-Frith premises of Sam Longson after the Company was absorbed into R Hanson & Son Ltd. It has a Gardner 180 and dates from 1974.

BRISTOL

Bristol Commercial Vehicles, Brislington, Bristol

Bristol eight wheelers were built exclusively for Road Haulage Executive (British Road Services) use, the nationalised road transport arm of the British Transport Commission. The Bristol Tramways & Carriage Co came under government control as part of the nationalisation of the rail and bus services which included the Tilling Group.

The RHE developed a standard long distance trunk vehicle to be used throughout the BRS network. The first HG6Ls, as they were designated, were unveiled in 1952 and had Leyland O.600 engines similar to the Leyland Octopus.

The RHE continued to place orders with existing manufacturers including Leyland, AEC, ERF, Foden, Atkinson and Albion. The Labour Government, who set up the BTC, fell from power in 1951 when the Tories were re-elected, only to begin the process of denationalisation. 321 of the original 22 ton Bristol HG6Ls were built before a redesigned 24 ton version also designated HG6L was introduced in 1956. 196 of these were built, production ceasing in 1958.

In accordance with the general shift towards articulation for long distance traffic Bristol switched their attention to the HA6G and HA6L tractor units, but sweeping changes in the Construction & Use Regulations in 1964 rendered the type obsolete. This combined with a diminishing role for BRS led to Bristol truck production ceasing altogether in 1964.

Above: FF12 is a Burlingham cabbed HG6L dating from 1953 and is seen here loaded and ready to set out from the BRS depot at Eastern Avenue, Dunstable, one cold winter's morning. The lorry began life at South Leicester branch wearing fleet number 41E674 before being transferred to Luton and Dunstable.

Right: HC36 swings out of Foster Street, Liverpool to head south along Bankhall Lane on a summer's day in July 1966. Registered XUM420 and bearing chassis number 124021 this is one of the later type HG6Ls with Longwell Green fibreglass cab and was based in the Tyne Tees district.

DODGE

Dodge Trucks, Dunstable, Bedfordshire

Dodge was never a significant player in the eight wheeler market but in conjunction with Unipower Ltd of Perivale they marketed a Dodge Unipower rigid eight from 1972 to 1974. They were based on the tilt cab 500 Series six wheelers. Dodge was the only mass-producer to enter the maximum weight multi-axle class.

Many operators in the Sixties had fourth axle conversions carried out on cheap mass-produced chassis such as Bedford, Ford, BMC and Dodge, suggesting that there was a market for lightweight, low-cost eight wheelers. The Dodge Unipower aimed to exploit that market.

In 1967 Chrysler, Dodge's parent company since the late Twenties, bought the Spanish Barreiros concern and renamed their products Dodge. Spanish Dodge 8x2 and 8x4 models were already operating in large numbers in their native country when it was decided to launch an Anglicised version on the UK market in 1978 – the 300 Series. Sales never reached large numbers and the model was withdrawn in 1982 after control of the UK operations was taken over by RVI (Renault Vehicules Industriels).

Above: Plated at 28 tons this Perkins V8-540 engined long wheelbase 500 Series Dodge Unipower K2413 eight wheeler with cage-side body for transporting bricks weighed in at under 9 tons unladen giving it an impressive payload capacity. New in 1974 it was operated by E H Lobb of Maulden before passing second-hand to A & F Motors of Flitwick.

Right: Camiones Barreiros of Madrid were absorbed into the Chrysler Corporation in 1967 and an Anglicised version of their popular Spanish rigid eight arrived on the UK scene as the Dodge 300 Series in 1978. This is a particularly good example owned by King's of Chelmsford. The cast spoke wheels are an interesting feature – British style disc wheels were standard.

ERF

ERF Ltd., Sandbach, Cheshire

ERF are one of the most significant eight wheeler manufacturers of all time having produced the type continuously since late 1934.

ERF was formed only one year before that by 'ER' (Edwin Richard) Foden, a member of the Foden family whose factory was just "up the road" at Elworth. 'ER' set up his new company with his son Dennis to build diesel engined lorries following internal arguments at Fodens over the respective merits of steam and diesel.

ERF rapidly grew to become a leading manufacturer of heavy vehicles. Their first eight wheeler, the CI6.8, was replaced by a completely new design, the 6.8, in 1947. This featured a stylish new V-front cab by Jennings Coachbuilders who were later taken over by ERF.

In 1954 the KV range with oval grille and wrap-round windscreen appeared, followed eight years later by the all fibreglass LV cabbed model. In many guises the LV continued in production until the launch of the tilt cab B-Series in 1974.

The B-Series had the revolutionary 'SP' (Steel/Plastics) cab. The design was so successful that the same basic cab technology is still employed on ERF's current truck range.

Above: Reliance Motors were the first to operate an ERF rigid eight back in 1935 and they remained faithful to the marque for many years. This V-type 6.8 with Gardner 6LW was delivered new to them in 1953. It has a 3300 gallon tank body, by Butterfields of Shipley.

Right: Successor to the V-type cab was the ultra-modern KV with its large wrap-round screens and distinctive oval grille. This one, in service with J M Watkins of Abergavenny, began life with a Cambridgeshire operator and was originally engaged on brick haulage. Watkins themselves regularly backloaded bricks from LBC Stewartby Works to South Wales having brought steel into Luton for Vauxhall Motors.

Left: Part fibreglass versions of the KV cab designated 2KV appeared in 1959. A typical example is this fine medium wheelbase 6.8GX tanker in service with Corn Products Company of Trafford Park, Manchester and used on the bulk distribution of sweeteners to the food industry. It was powered by a Gardner 6LX.

Right: Perhaps the best looking version of the KV cab was this – the 2KV12. It was fitted to eight wheelers and four wheelers with set-back front axles. This example photographed at Alf Whitehouse's yard at Cheswardine, Market Drayton, appears to have been fitted with a later ERF badge from a mid-Sixties LV.

Left: In 1962 ERF launched the LV cabbed range with its large single-piece curved windscreen. Early versions were by Boalloy of Congleton who were responsible for the design of the cab. Soon Jennings of Sandbach were supplying LV cabs, identifiable by their round wheelarches. The 1962 Boalloy version seen here in the fleet of G Earnshaw of Blaxton, Doncaster, had slightly squared wheelarches.

Above: This Jennings LV cabbed tanker, dating from 1964, was one of a number operated by Valentin Ord & Nagle of Bletchley, Bucks. It was powered by a Gardner 6LX. The Jennings cabs had smaller front access panels than the Boalloy versions.

Left: Another fine example of the Jennings LV, in this case a 1965 6.8GX medium wheelbase chassis with 'pencil' tank for the transport of corrosive liquids. It belonged to the large tanker fleet of Smith & Robinson, Oulton Lane, Rothwell near Leeds.

Right: The LV cab design spanned about 12 years with numerous detail modifications. This is a 1969 6LV/L (the L suffix indicating an illuminated built-in headboard). It was part of a large ERF fleet operated by Gordon Plant, then based at North Rode, Macclesfield.

Left: Final version of the LV was the 8LV launched in 1970. This 1970 long wheelbase bulk powder tanker belonged to British Salt who are based at Middlewich, not far from the town of Sandbach where it was built. Power unit is the Gardner 6LX '150'.

Above: Versions with set back front axles took the 7LV cab. This is a late one dating from 1975. It shared the same external appearance as the A-Series. This nicely liveried 30 ton gross example belonged to H D Fraser of Conon Bridge which lies to the north of Inverness. It was powered by a Cummins 220 making it a powerful machine for the period.

Left: Successor to the LV cabbed eight wheeler was the tilt cab B-Series launched in 1974. The majority went for tipper use but some found their way into long distance haulage like this impressive fridge van in the livery of Thornhill Meat Packers of Great Longstone in Derbyshire. It was powered by a 6LXB '180' and grossed 30 tons.

Above: Also sporting a '180' is this superb eight wheel flat of Layton & Steele, Bloxwich. This 1977 31G 4RD is seen loaded with approximately 20 tons of steel in the form of two large coils.

FODEN

Fodens Ltd., Sandbach, Cheshire

Foden's long history goes back to 1856 but until the early Thirties the company was mainly concerned with steam vehicles. Though reluctant to accept the supremacy of internal combustion, Fodens were on the diesel lorry scene from 1931 and produced a small number of eight wheelers as early as 1934.

Their first, the 'R type', was a heavily built machine based on their six wheeler but with a second steering axle. It had Kirkstall rear axles like the Speed Twelve steamer.

However, the first purpose designed rigid eight was the 'DG' which appeared in 1935. It featured the ubiquitous Gardner 6LW oil engine, a four-speed gearbox and Foden's own overhead worm axles. The stylish S2 'Airstream' cab was very modern in appearance for the Thirties. A flat radiator was fitted.

A re-designed DG appeared in 1937, having a curved radiator and was a familiar sight through to the introduction of the FG/FE range in 1948. This had a smart new cab, the S18, with concealed radiator. During the Fifties Foden became established as one of the leading eight wheeler manufacturers.

A variety of cab types appeared over the next three decades including the S24 tilt cab - the first to be offered on a British heavy lorry. Their last eight wheeler offering before being taken over by Paccar in 1980 was the S10-cabbed Haulmaster. Foden still commands a leading position in the UK eight wheeler market.

Above: Spanning two generations of Foden eight wheelers this shot, taken in Joseph Roscoe's yard at Westhoughton, Lancs, shows a 1947 DG6/15 standing next to a 1950 registered FG6/15. It highlights the big advance made in cab styling with the launch of the FG in 1948 although MTD would have had a flat fronted cab originally. It was most likely replaced with a 'V' front around 1954. Note the 40x8 wheels and exquisite signwriting befitting a traditional Lancashire haulier of Roscoe's standing. CBN602 was one of the last DGs engaged on long distance general haulage and operated mainly between Lancashire and Scotland.

Right: Capturing the grimy industrial environment in which many lorries operated this photograph depicts a flat front S18-cabbed FG6/15 of Magnet Transport, Sheffield. It is a 1951 model and began life with the Cement Marketing Company as Fleet No.841.

ft: With its 1952 Hereford
gistration this V front FE6/15
o-stroke was probably new to
der makers H P Bulmer but is
en here in the splendid livery
F Wardell (Haulage) Ltd of
mm, Cheshire. Nothing can
ompare with the sound of an
06 'stroker' in full song.

Above: The S20 saloon cab with its four piece wrap-round windscreen brought new elegance to the Foden range from 1956. This fine example from the fleet of A Pannell, Golders Green is seen loaded with a 'Lancashire' flat carrying sheet steel.

Left: 1958 saw the introduction of the S21, popularly known today as the Mickey Mouse. This 1962 registered example was one of a large fleet of liquid carbon dioxide tankers operated by ICI from Billingham-on-Tees.

Above: Simmons Watts, part of RHM Agricultural Ltd, were the operators of this impressive 1965 'Mouse' 26-ton gvw tipper for bulk feed. The vehicle was 13 years old when this picture was taken, bearing testimony to the durability of the fibreglass S21 cab.

Left: Tilt cabs first appeared in the 1962 range and Foden was the first British manufacturer to offer them. Designated the S24, identifiable by its oblong headlamps, single piece windscreen and the absence of a removable front grille, the new cab was of ultra modern appearance for the time. The 1966 bulk tipper shown here was part of a well known Foden fleet operated by Selby's Garage, Woodhouse, Leics.

Right: Facelifted versions of the S24 cab came along in 1967. The tilt version became the S34 while a fixed version was dubbed the S36. Both had slant mounted four headlamp systems and a slightly deeper windscreen than the S24. The Albion Sugar Co. of Woolwich were well known Foden users who were noted for their streamlined glucose tankers but this 1967 model has a high sided dropside body.

ALBION SUGAR Co. Ltd
ALBION SUGAR Co. Ltd
BREWING SUGARS
GLUCOSE SYRUPS
63
RGO 229E

Left: Half cabs were another Foden speciality, first appearing on dumpers in the Fifties. This is an example of their later S50 half cab as fitted to a 1970 24-ton gross tipper of the ARC Group.

Right: Also in ARC livery is this 1972 30-ton gross tipper from their South Western Division and operating out of their quarry at Helston, Cornwall. It features the updated fibreglass cab in S39 form which was a non tilt version with split windscreen first introduced in 1969.

Left: Foden introduced more cab variants than most other manufacturers, different types often overlapping by some years. The S80 tilt cab, instantly recognisable by its large headlamps, first appeared in 1972. This Rolls Royce Eagle powered 30-ton gross machine entered the Morning Foods fleet in 1975 and was photographed when barely a week old. The company, who manufacture Mornflake porridge oats, boasted an immaculately kept fleet of eight wheelers in this attractive pale turquoise and red livery.

Right: Foden's last eight wheeler offering prior to the Paccar takeover in 1980 was the S10 Haulmaster. It was launched in 1978 and was the best seller in the Foden range at that time. It had many chassis refinements including the availability of Foden's own FF20 rubber rear suspension. Rolls and Cummins engines were rapidly taking precedence over Gardner but this London Brick Company vehicle, seen here fully laden at their Stewartby Works, featured the traditional Patricroft built engine. It is a trailing axle model with conventional steel four-spring rear bogie.

GUY

Guy Motors Ltd., Wolverhampton, Staffordshire

Traditionally Guy Motors had only built four and six wheeled lorries prior to 1954 when they launched their Invincible range based on the AEC Mammoth Major Mk.III. Initially it was called the Goliath but this old Guy model name had by then been adopted by a German van builder so they had to relinquish it.

By 1958 Guy had developed their own chassis with Kirkstall axles and a new ultra modern cab with large wrap-round windscreen. It was launched as the Invincible Mk.2. The following year a lightweight model was added, powered by an AEC AVU470 engine and dubbed the Warrior Light Eight.

Guy became part of Jaguar Cars in 1961 and in 1964 a newly developed eight wheeler was launched as the Big J8. The range was noted for its wide choice of engines but the main power unit was initially a Cummins V6 with a choice of 170 or 200 bhp rating. Cummins V engines were by then in full production at their Darlington factory. Optional engines included Gardner, AEC and Leyland.

The Guy Big J8 continued in production with various modifications up to 1979. A 30-ton version was introduced in 1972 and became the popular choice of many tipper operators.

Above: Heading north up Archway Hill on a summer's evening this Boalloy cabbed Guy Invincible Mk.1 served in the fleet of W H Bowker of Blackburn. The Mk.1 was virtually identical to the AEC Mk.III but for its Gardner 6LW engine and David Brown gearbox. A Meadows engine was optional. This nicely liveried machine dates from 1959.

Right: Sharing the same cab design as the Invincible Mk.2 the Warrior Light Eight introduced in 1959 was powered by an AEC AVU470 diesel and was popular with operators seeking maximum payload capacity. Fletchers of Ibstock, who specialised in the haulage of coal and coke, had this one new in 1966.

Left: General & Industrial Paints of Perivale, Middlesex, were the operators of this 1967 24-ton gross Big J8 which was Guy's new eight wheeler introduced following the Jaguar takeover. The standard power unit was the Cummins V6-170 but a wide range of engines was available. The cab was a Motor Panels steel construction shared with Seddon, Scammell, Foden and ERF.

Right: A later Gardner engined 30-ton gross Guy Big J8 owned by R E Mason who, like their associate company Fletchers of Ibstock, were coal hauliers, but based at Kilsby near Rugby. The Big J range was phased out in the late Seventies as part of Leyland Truck & Bus Division's rationalisation.

LEYLAND

Leyland Motors Ltd., Leyland, Lancashire

In 1935 Leyland Motors added a second steering axle to a Hippo six wheeler and the Octopus was born. It went on to become one of the most famous of all eight wheelers. The pre war type, designated TEW, was replaced after the war by the new 22.O/1 and 22.O/3 (SWB) with modernised cab and completely re-engineered chassis, on the scene by 1947.

In the mid Fifties a re-designed cab (56/A) was introduced and an increase in the UK legal weight to 24 tons brought the 24.O/4 and 24.O/5 models. The LAD 'Power Plus' range appeared in 1960.

Throughout the Fifties and Sixties the Leyland empire was growing rapidly, absorbing numerous other manufacturers. By the late Sixties Leyland owned AEC, Albion, Guy, Maudslay, Scammell and Thornycroft, all of whom had been important eight wheeler manufacturers.

A major rationalisation programme was necessary to simplify the range and many of the once famous marques disappeared in the ensuing years. By the late Seventies Leyland Truck & Bus had killed off virtually all the above mentioned makes and were about to launch their new Constructor range which was developed by Scammell. The name 'Octopus' was dropped when the Octopus 2 was discontinued in 1980.

Above: The short wheelbase tipper version of the 22.O/1 was designated the 22.O/3. This one, in operation with Blackpool based quarry owners Keirby & Perry bears a 1950 London registration and was still hard at work in the mid Sixties.

Right: The first new post war eight wheeler from Leyland was the 22.O/1, powered by the 9.8 litre O.600 oil engine. The 600 Series cab, though plain and simple, was a great classic of its era. They were built of steel or aluminium according to the customers' preference and, to some extent, material supply. They were very popular as fuel tankers.

Left: British Road Services placed large orders for Octopuses throughout the Fifties and considerable numbers were based at depots throughout the UK. The biggest concentration was in South Wales but there were also large numbers based in East Anglia, including Peterborough and Whittlesey, where they were mainly engaged on work for the London Brick Co.

Right: In the Midlands fleet of A C Horton, a susidiary of Andrew Wishart of Dysart, Kircaldy, this beautifully liveried 24.O/4 dropsider was engaged on transport of linoleum for Nairn Floorings. Though mechanically similar in most respects to the earlier 22.O/1s it featured air brakes.

Left: One of the last operators to run a sizeable fleet of Leyland Octopus 24.O/4s was Hipwood & Grundy of Farnworth near Bolton. Their tankers were engaged on fuel oil distribution. This 1956 model was photographed at their depot as late as 1973.

Above: In 1960 the Octopus took on a completely new guise with the 'LAD' steel cab by Motor Panels. Next to the earlier 600 Series the new cab, shared with Albion and Dodge, lacked interior space. Nevertheless the 'LAD' Octopus is a classic of its era and, with its choice of 140 bhp 'O.600' or 200 bhp 'O.680' Power Plus diesels, boasted a much improved performance over its predecessors. This one, a 1962 model, had put in a lot of hard work with Taylors of Lichfield when this photograph was taken in 1968.

Above: H B & H were noted for their impressive Power Plus eight wheelers and trailers during the Sixties. This typical example, registered in 1963, was photographed at their yard in Newton-le-Willows, Lancashire. The Power Plus range had a relatively short reign.

Right: In 1964 the LAD was replaced by the new tilt cab 'Ergomatic' Freightline range. The new cab, designed by Michelotti, marked a significant step forward. Heavy Transport, part of the ECC Group, were still operating a number of old 24.O/5 tippers when this 'Ergo' joined the fleet in 1966.

Left: With weight increases introduced in 1964 eight wheelers were allowed to gross up to 26 and 28 tons depending on axle spread. Not many were built at 28 tons since the required 26ft outer axle spread was too long to be practical. Leyland did however offer a 26 ton Octopus on a 20ft 9in. wheelbase.
This is an example at work with J W Walker & Sons in Liverpool.

Right: One operator who stayed loyal to the Leyland Octopus was Southern Cross Transport Ltd of Hatfield. Even when Leylands had officially pulled out of the eight wheeler market through declining sales, Southern Cross insisted on ordering new Octopuses which Leyland obligingly built. Some were supplied as late as 1974. Many ex-Southern Cross Octopuses were bought by owner-drivers in the Bedfordshire area where local brick and block manufacturers provided ample work. This 1973 'Ergo' was photographed unloading blocks at a housing development in Flitwick in 1980.

Left: After a period of withdrawal from the eight wheeler market between 1970 and 1975 Leyland re-entered the scene with the new lightweight Octopus with restyled cab and fixed head 502 diesel. The more powerful 511 engine was added in 1976. This 1979 example was part of the large Redland fleet.

Right: In 1978 Leyland announced their Octopus 2 powered by the TL11 turbo. This tipper went into service with Frimstone of Kings Lynn at the beginning of 1981. By that time Leyland had launched their completely new Routeman based 'Constructor' 8 wheeler The photograph was taken at Dickerson's quarry in Waterbeach, Cambridgeshire.

MAUDSLAY

Maudslay Motor Co., Coventry, Warwickshire

Based at Coventry and Alcester in Warwickshire the Maudslay Motor Company entered the eight wheeler market in the first months of World War Two with their Mikado – an 'assembled' vehicle which, like the Atkinson and ERF, had a Gardner/David Brown/Kirkstall driveline. Only a handful of Mikados were built in the 1939-41 period.

After the war a new model, the Meritor, was launched, powered by an AEC 9.6 litre engine driving through a David Brown 5-speed gearbox to Maudslay built Kirkstall pattern rear axles. They were built as double drive models with third differential.

A short wheelbase tipper version was also offered, but only six were ever built. AEC owned Maudslay from 1948 and from 1950 began building Mk.III eight wheelers with Maudslay radiator badges. Their chassis numbers were prefixed 'M'.

Just 256 long wheelbase Meritors were built, many of which were ordered by the Road Haulage Executive for BRS. They were popular as trailer models. The Maudslay name was discontinued from 1958.

Above: Maudslay Meritor eight wheelers were diminishing in numbers in the 1960s and only a handful were still operational when this example was photographed in Birmingham in 1966. It had spent all its working life with the Maudslay Motor Company, operating on general trade plates. Still in its Maudslay works colours it had been purchased by F P R Cranes of Handsworth for hauling tackle. Shortly after this it was bought by the author for preservation and appears in restored form on the back cover of this book.

Right: Many Meritors ended their days with travelling showmen. This example, a 1950 model bearing chassis number 85206, operated with BRS parcels at Dewsbury carrying fleet number P50D852. It retained its Tillotson cab and Luton body while with Marshall's Amusements of Bradford.

HD·8938

81

SCAMMELL

Scammell Lorries Ltd., Watford, Hertfordshire

Scammells are often looked upon as the archetypal Rigid Eights. Indeed they introduced the term to distinguish their rigid eight wheeler from their main product, the Artic Eight. However Scammell did not fully enter the eight wheeler market until 1937 and when they did it was with a highly unconventional design with a unique load-compensating front bogie.

They were noted for their exceptionally light weight even though they presented a very solid appearance. The original model with its Gardner 6LW, Scammell 6-speed overdrive gear box and unusual epicyclic double reduction axle continued in production until 1958 when it was replaced by a more modern version with fibreglass cab, the Routeman I.

Very soon the Routeman I was replaced by a completely new model, the Routeman II with its striking Michelotti cab. It first appeared in 1962. It was a successful design but was only offered in 8x2 form. It became even more successful when the 8x4 Routeman III with Albion rear axles appeared in 1968. Tipper operators swore by it and in its later 30 ton gross form it provided the basis for Leyland's new Constructor of 1980.

Above: The Scammell Rigid Eight embodied many unique engineering features and boasted one of the lowest unladen weights in the business. This example dates from 1950 and is seen in the Accrington Brick and Tile livery but was on contract to them from T Bolton of Accrington. The first operators were Guinness at Park Royal.

Right: Between the Rigid Eight and the familiar Michelotti-cabbed Routeman II Scammell built a small number of Routeman I models mainly with Gardner engines. This 1959 example was one of a number in the fleet of United Molasses, based in Liverpool.

Left: The Routeman II retained much of Scammell's in-house engineering, including their 6-speed gate-change gearbox and epicyclic drive axle. All were built as trailing axle machines until 1968 when the double drive Routeman III with Albion Reiver hub reduction axles was introduced. This is a 1965 8x2 from the Esso Petroleum fleet.

Above: Though not ideal for on-off road work the Routeman II 8x2 found its way into some tipper fleets like this one operated by Oliver Hart of Coppull, Lancs. It is a 1966 model with high-sided body for bulk coal.

Left: Once the Routeman III 8x4 was introduced in 1968 tipper sales gained ground considerably and they were used in many branches of the construction business. This is one of a large nationally-based fleet of 24 ton gross bulk cement tankers once in service with Blue Circle Cement.

Right: The 30 ton gross Routeman III soon became the leading choice of many tipper fleets in the Seventies. This is a classic example from the fleet of I T Thomas & Sons, based at Kidwelly in South Wales. It dates from 1975 and is powered by the 202bhp Leyland O.680. The Rolls Royce Eagle 220 was also available in this model.

SEDDON

Seddon Motors Ltd., Oldham, Lancashire

Seddon Motors of Oldham were late-comers to the eight wheeler scene. They surprised the industry with a completely new model, the SD8/DD8 (single or double drive) in 1958. It was built on very conventional lines having a choice of Gardner or Cummins engine. AEC engines could also be fitted to special order for certain customers. They were available in long (17ft 9in) or short (14ft 6in) wheelbase form.

In 1962 a re-engineered model was put on the market with a more modern cab featuring four headlamps and a single-piece windscreen.

The shrinking demand for rigid eights resulting from pro-artic legislation in 1964 led Seddon to pull out of the market in that year. In doing so they appeared to have no plans to develop heavier eight wheelers at 26 or 28 tons to take advantage of the new legislation. Instead they concentrated on heavy tractor units.

However, following the takeover of Atkinson, they re-entered the eight wheeler market as Seddon Atkinson (see pages 90 & 91). Their 400 Series drew its engineering mainly from the highly successful Atkinson Defender but in 1980 the lightweight 300 Series owed more to Seddon's own design team.

Above: Seddon Motors of Oldham launched their DD8 and SD8 models in 1958. This SD8 (single drive) was one of three latex tankers based at the British Vita plant in Middleton near Manchester. They operated at 24 tons gross but had a design weight of 28 tons. Power unit was a Gardner 6LX '150'.

Right: Within four years of their launch the original SD8/DD8s were replaced by the new 24-8-6LX and 24-DD8-6LX models with restyled cab and a new design of fully-articulating two-spring rear bogie. They were highly successful machines but the whole future of 24 ton gross eight wheelers was threatened after pro-artic weight legislation was introduced in 1964. This 1963 tanker is in the livery of GLS Transport who were bulk liquid hauliers based at Whetstone in North London. It carries a 4,000 gallon Steel Barrel Co. tank body.

SEDDON ATKINSON

Seddon Atkinson Vehicles Ltd., Oldham Lancashire

Seddon Motors bought Atkinson in 1970 forming Seddon Atkinson from 1971. Shortly after, in 1974, that company was taken over by International Harvester. In 1975 the first joint products were dubbed Seddon Atkinson 400s, the eight wheeler version being inspired mainly by Atkinson's Defender but having the advantage of an ultra-modern tilt cab.

In 1980 a lightweight eight wheeler, the 300 Series, was launched, powered by an International Harvester 466 turbo-charged diesel. Initially Seddon Atkinsons featured a new design of 'entwined circles' badge representing the linking of Seddon and Atkinson but in 1981 the much respected 'Big A' badge was reinstated on all models.

From 1986 the heavier duty eight wheelers, by then badged as '401', were discontinued. The 301 followed by the updated 311 continued until the introduction of the new Strato eight wheelers in 1990.

Now part of the Iveco Group, Seddon Atkinson remain a significant force in the UK eight wheeler market.

Left: Among the early Seddon Atkinson 400 Series eight wheelers to enter service was this nicely liveried bulk grain tipper from the fleet of Charles & Co (Leith) Ltd. It was photographed on the outskirts of Edinburgh when new in 1975.

Above: The International engined 300 Series lightweight eight wheeler appeared in 1980. Many operators disliked the rather anonymous 'entwined circles' badge and some chose to fit their own Big A badges. This early 300 belonged to T H Smith of Rawnsley near Cannock.

THORNYCROFT

Transport Equipment (Thornycroft) Ltd., Basingstoke, Hampshire

The old established Basinstoke firm of Thornycroft planned to introduce an eight wheeler in 1940 but the war intervened and they did not enter the market until late in 1946. Their PF/NR6 Trusty was a heavily built machine employing mainly in house running units. The only exception being Kirkstall rear axles.

The early Trustys were powered by the 100bhp 7.88 litre NR6/MV diesel and had a two-stick 5-speed (4 plus overdrive 5th) gearbox. Later 'PFs' had direct top 5-speed boxes.

A new model, the PK/QR6 was launched at the 1956 Earls Court Show and entered production in 1957. This had a stylish new cab and a more powerful 9.83 litre diesel developing 130bhp plus other mechanical refinements which earned it favourable press reports.

After only four years or so PK production ceased as AEC bought Thornycroft in 1961, and the model clashed with AEC's own Mammoth Major. In 1960 a new Thornycroft eight wheeler, the T8, was under development but only a couple of prototypes were built, at least one of which was operated on the works' own transport fleet.

Above: Thornycroft Trusty eight wheelers were never produced in the same large volumes as AEC and Leyland but quite a number entered service with BRS in the Fifties. This 1953 PF/NR6/MV, now preserved*, was once based in the Southampton area.

*This photograph, unlike all others in this book, was taken in 1995. The vehicle had undergone a complete rebuild by brothers Len and Bob Nield from Manchester and is easily the most accurately restored lorry in the UK.

Right: AEC took over Thornycroft in 1961, just four years after they launched their new, improved eight wheeler – the PK/QR6. Old established J W Watts of Beverley in East Yorks was among the well known long distance hauliers who operated the type. This one was photographed in Hull and dates from 1960.

CLASSIC EIGHT WHEELERS

These scale side view line drawings give an at-a-glance view of sixteen of Britain's best known rigid eights from the Fifties and Sixties. At approximately 1/96th full size they form a useful reference for model makers as well as an interesting comparison between the various model types.

1

2

3

4

5

6

7

8

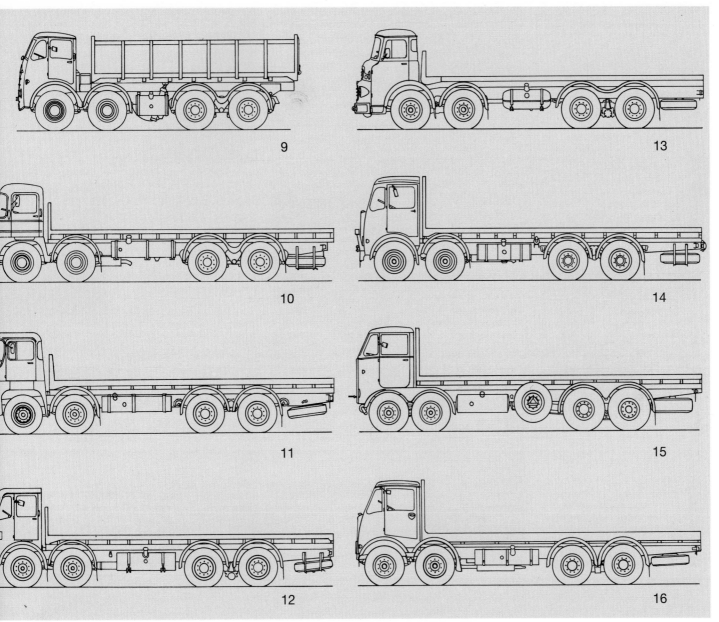

1. 1952 AEC 3871 Mammoth Major Mk. III, 18ft 9½in. w/b. (BRS)

2. 1962 AEC G8RA Mammoth Major Mk. V, 17ft 4½in. w/b.

3. 1966 AEC TG8R Ergomatic Mammoth Major, 17ft 2in w/b.

4. 1950 Albion CX7N, 18ft 3in w/b.

5. 1950 Atkinson L1586, 17ft 8¼ w/b.

6. 1956 Bristol HG6L, 18ft 0in w/b. (BRS)

7. 1950 ERF 6.8 'V-type', 18ft 0in w/b.

8. 1956 ERF 6.8G 'KV', 18ft 0in w/b.

9. 1954 Foden FG6/15 'S18', 14ft 3½in w/b. tipper.

10. 1960 Foden KG6/24 'S21' (Mickey Mouse), 18ft 1¼in w/b.

11. 1959 Guy Invincible Mk.2, 17ft 9in w/b.

12. 1952 Leyland 22.0/1 Octopus, 17ft 9in w/b.

13. 1960 Leyland 24.0/11R 'LAD' Power Plus Octopus, 17ft 0in w/b.

14. 1950 Maudslay Meritor, 17ft 6in w/b (BRS)

15. 1950 Scammell 'Rigid Eight' 19ft 0in w/b.

16. 1953 Thornycroft PF/NR6/MV 18ft 4in w/b.

Note:
Whilst every effort has been made to ensure accuracy, the drawings shown can only serve as a general guide for model makers. Precision can only be guaranteed by working from larger scale drawings.

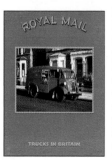

ROYAL MAIL This Trucks in Britain book takes as its subject the familiar red vehicles - past and present - of the GPO, Royal Mail, Parcelforce. Also includes specialist vehicles including postbuses, motorbikes and combinations, TV detector vans, security vehicles & tugs. 80p. 32 colour & 150 mono illustrations. s/b. £9.95 h/b. £12.95

AEC LORRIES In The Post War Years 1945-1979 *Graham Edge.* An illustrated history tracing the rise, consolidation and sad decline of the Southall manufacturer enhanced by over 200 mono & colour photographs of AECs in both civilian & military guise and at home & abroad. 152p. h/b. £19.95

ERF - 'The World's Best Oil Engined Lorry' *Peter Davies* turns the clock back for a nostalgic look at six decades of ERF, recalling the company's history and growth and the development of its vehicles into the 90s. 128p. 258 mono & colour illustrations. h/b. £19.95

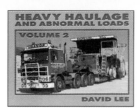

HEAVY HAULAGE & ABNORMAL LOADS Volume 2 *David Lee* presents a new photographic selection of colour & mono images of Heavy Haulage outfits and their loads seen operating during the period 1970 - 1994. 176p. 174 colour & mono illustrations. h/b £18.95

THE STORY OF PICKFORDS: *Arthur Ingram* reveals the development of Pickfords transport undertakings - removals, parcel traffic, meat haulage, contract hire, heavy haulage and even coaching operations which existed under differing ownerships. 112 pages, 180 mono illustrations h/b. £15.95

WHITBREAD: 250 YEARS OF BREWERY TRANSPORT *Arthur Ingram.* An informative illustrated history of Whitbread's transport vehicles by Arthur Ingram, a former employee of many years standing within the company's transport operations. 180 mono & colour illustrations. 96p. h/b. £15.95

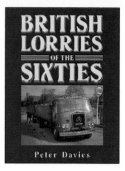

BRITISH LORRIES OF THE SIXTIES *Peter Davies.* Features a period when fundamental changes to the road traffic regulations had a profound effect on the type of lorry that would be required to meet the needs of the new Motorway era. 128p. Over 200 mono & colour illustrations. h/b. £18.95

BRITISH LORRIES of the 40s & 50s *Peter Davies'* popular book on the heyday of the British lorry manufacturer, with the post-war lorry presented at work in its natural environment, chronicled under the chapter headings of 4, 6, 8 wheelers and artic. vehicles. 200 superb mono & colour illustrations. 128p. h/b. £17.95

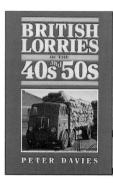

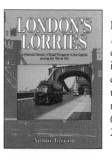

LONDON'S LORRIES *Arthur Ingram's* personal tour of the capital city, presenting a host of varied and interesting light & heavy commercial vehicles from all over the country which were to be found on its roads and streets during the 50s & 60s. 144 pages of pure nostalgia! 285 mono illustrations h/b. £16.95